LIFE IN THE — U.S. — ARMY

by Mo Barrett

PEBBLE
a capstone imprint

Published by Pebble, an imprint of Capstone
1710 Roe Crest Drive, North Mankato, Minnesota 56003
capstonepub.com

Library of Congress Cataloging-in-Publication Data is available on the Library of Congress website.

ISBN: 9780756579883 (hardcover)
ISBN: 9780756580001 (paperback)
ISBN: 9780756579982 (ebook PDF)

Summary: Gives readers a peak into daily life for U.S. Army soldiers.

Editorial Credits
Editor: Mandy Robbins; Designer: Heidi Thompson; Media Researcher: Jo Miller;
Production Specialist: Tori Abraham

Image Credits
Getty Images: xavierarnau, 21; Shutterstock: HENX, 6, Picksell, background (throughout); U.S. Air Force photo by Airman 1st Class Joseph Garcia, 15, Tech. Sgt. Duncan McElroy, 4; U.S. Army photo by 1st Lt. Ryan DeBooy, 14, Alexandra Shea, Fort Jackson Public Affairs Office, 19, Capt. Adam Weece, Cover (top middle), Capt. Eric Connor, 10, Capt. William Stroud, 5, Cpl. Gun Woo Song, Cover (bottom), Pvt. Michael Bradle, 7, Scott T. Sturkol, Public Affairs Office, Fort McCoy, Wis., 17, Sgt. Amanda Tucker, 9, Spc. L'Erin Wynn, 11, Staff Sgt. Angela S. Kim/1st Security Force Assistance Brigade, 13, Staff Sgt. Nicholaus Williams, Cover (top left), Steven Stover, Cover (top right)

Printed and bound in China. 5834

TABLE OF CONTENTS

Words in **bold** appear in the glossary.

BRAVE SOLDIERS

U.S. Army soldiers defend America on the ground and beyond. They protect our country during times of war.

They also help people when there are emergencies. They bring food, water, and other supplies.

Soldiers load supplies for earthquake victims.

WHAT SOLDIERS WEAR

Soldiers wear special **uniforms**. They include patches or pins with a soldier's name on it. The soldier's name is also on a piece of metal that they wear like a necklace. Soldiers call them **dog tags** because they look like ID tags worn by dogs.

Blank dog tags

STARTING THE DAY

A **bugle** sounds at 7:00 a.m. It tells soldiers to get up and start the day! The notes in a bugle call are messages. One call tells soldiers it is time to eat. At the end of the day, another call tells them it is time for bed.

Fitness is important in the army. Soldiers must be ready for physical challenges. Once a day, they do warm-ups and exercises. Soldiers run. They do pushups and pull-ups. They might even do an **obstacle course**.

A DAY'S WORK

After exercising, soldiers stand in **formation**. Officers make sure all the soldiers are wearing clean uniforms. They give soldiers important information about what they will be doing at work that day.

After formation, soldiers train. They prepare for **combat** situations. They might shoot weapons or drive tanks or trucks. They work with other soldiers to build their skills.

Soldiers have different jobs. They can be **engineers**, doctors, **mechanics**, or pilots. The Army even has veterinarians to care for military dogs and horses.

WHERE SOLDIERS LIVE

Soldiers work at special places called **posts**. They are like small cities. A post has houses and parks. It has stores and even police and fire departments.

Some soldiers live on the post with their families. Others live nearby and drive to their post for work. The Army protects American interests everywhere. Army posts are all over the world.

Fort McCoy, Wisconsin

A SOLDIER'S GREETING

Soldiers greet each other by saying, "Hooah!" It sounds funny, but it is like a greeting for a special club. No one knows exactly how this saying started. It can mean "Yes," "I understand," or even "How are you?" Try saying it—*HOOAH*!

EXERCISE LIKE A SOLDIER

Obstacle courses help soldiers stay fit and ready for anything. Create your own obstacle course!

Warm up first. Stretch and do 10 jumping jacks.

- **Low crawl:** Set up strings between two chairs that you have to crawl under.

- **Balance beam:** Draw a line on the sidewalk that you have to walk along.

- **Hoop hop:** Lay hula hoops on the ground to hop into and out of.

GLOSSARY

bugle (BYOO-guhl)—a trumpet without keys

combat (KOM-bat)—fighting between people or armies

dog tag (DAHG TAG)—a metal identification tag, worn on a chain around the neck

engineer (en-juh-NEER)—someone trained to design and build machines, vehicles, bridges, roads, or other structures

formation (for-MAY-shuhn)—the way in which members of a group are arranged

mechanic (muh-KAN-ik)—someone who fixes vehicles or machinery

obstacle course (OB-stuh-kuhl KORSS)—a series of barriers that soldiers must jump over, climb, or crawl through

post (POHST)—an area run by the Army where people serving in the military live and military supplies are stored

uniform (YOU-nuh-form)—special clothing that members of a particular group wear

READ MORE

Engler, Lisa. *Lil' Army Soldier*. New York: Running Press Kids, 2020.

Pallotta, Jerry, and Sammie Garnett. *US Army Alphabet Book*. Watertown, MA: Charlesbridge Publishing, 2021.

Vonder Brink, Tracy. *The United States Army*. North Mankato, MN: Pebble, 2021.

INTERNET SITES

Britannica Kids: Army
kids.britannica.com/kids/article/army/352785

Sesame Street for Military Families
sesamestreetformilitaryfamilies.org

United States Army Facts for Kids
kids.kiddle.co/United_States_Army

INDEX

ABOUT THE AUTHOR

Mo Barrett is a retired Colonel. She spent nearly 30 years in the Air Force flying as a pilot and setting up airfields. She is now a public speaker and entertainer, using humor to change the way people laugh, learn, and think.